Wonder Uprising

RELATIONAL INTIMACY EDITION

A *personal* guidebook
to retrieve wholeheartedness
and uplift our relational selves

**CAROL DELMONICO
& CASEY DAVIS**

ARTWORK BY JESS DEMONTE

To the seekers,
to the relators, and
to the forgotten ways of knowing
that weave our relationships.

We honor and acknowledge the more than human world
for all the teachings it offers.

Table of Contents

Hello,
Friend...

Welcome! *We are so excited you are here!* This edition of **Wonder upRising** is deep and wide like a river. You can swim in the currents and eddies, rapids and narrowings. You can pause and sit on the bank. Bask in what you are discovering. Give your tears to the waters. Let go of what isn't needed. Embrace what is. And slide back in for more.

And...

I don't know about you, but me, sometimes more often than I'd like to admit, I feel lonelier with people than when I am by myself. Feeling lonely is one thing. Feeling lonely with others is a whole 'nother kind of loneliness.

My sense is that I'm not alone in the loneliness. And I'm not solitary in wondering what has gone awry in a world where relationships are relegated to the backdoor of our lives, the things we'll take care of when the "important stuff" is done. Productivity and its best friend, busyness. Interactions that sound like, *"How are you? I'm fine. Wanna have a beer? Let's binge watch Netflix together or talk about the football game. Maybe go shopping?"* only go so far to satisfy. Many of the habitual ways common in the dominant culture leave me hankering for alone time, in nature, to remember that loneliness is a people problem.

We've shared these pages with friends and family before we offered them up to the world. They gave them a thumbs up and five stars! The first question on acknowledgement led to changes in my relationship with my partner, Kevin. We do acknowledgements daily now and see each other with ever changing eyes. It's about practice not perfection and it's added a level of knowing we wouldn't have without it. And we (Casey and I) have grown our own relational intimacy so much deeper and wider, more than we could have ever imagined as we began this creative endeavor together.

Betwixt and between the pages of this book is the magic of witnessing yourself. This work comes from our deep belief that each of us, individually and collectively, can express more love.
And if not now, when?

We know there are a lot of relationship books and experts. Far be that from us. We are full time wonderers. And if you wonder a lot, questions become a way of mapping the world with beauty and curiosity. And answers become a way of navigating the forest, the ground they walk on.

We believe in you.

In your ability to access
your own inner wisdom.
Your shadow and your light.
Your gifts,
your values,
your generosity,
your care, and
your love.
All of it.

This is a resource that believes you have the
capacity and the tenacity to mine your own life.
Because discernment is not for the elite or special.
It lives in **all of us.**

Explore your past.
Your habits of thinking.
Your history and how it's reflected in the present.
Your desires.
Your fears.
How you co-mingle.
How you understand or not.
Where your blindspots lie.
And imagine your way into delightful, meaningful moments.
Together and apart.

It invites you into a space to _WONDER_.
To ponder. And consider. And rise up.

Stay connected,

Carol + Casey

This book has a companion:
the Shared Guidebook

If you are in partnership or have a close relationship with
someone that you'd like to grow, we encourage you to ask
them to join you in this practice using their own *Personal
Guidebook.* If they say *'yes'*, schedule a consistent time bimonthly or monthly to exchange and reflect upon answers to
the questions together using the *Shared Guidebook*.

The *Shared Guidebook* **is a place to come together.** It contains the same
questions as the *Personal Guidebook*, yet moves partners through a
different set of prompts. It is a space to imagine a new, more connecting
path forward together.

The *Personal Guidebook* **can be done alone, or in tandem with the**
Shared Guidebook. Either way, you will reap many gifts that you can then
bring into your relationships by using this workbook privately.

The Fourth R: Relationships

We place a lot of attention on the 3 R's in schools, but where in the dominant culture is the attention on *Relationships*? The R that holds all the other R's and everything else together seems to be absent from our list of cultural learning. The impact of this omission is deep and wide because what is left out of formal systems is often devalued.

We are not suggesting that educational systems take this on.

We simply want to acknowledge, and be curious about the possibility that the value of relational intimacy has been diminished when left to its own devices for being disseminated. And that has had, and continues to have, an impact on the well-being of humans and the more than human world. We are relational beings after all!

This edition of Wonder upRising focuses on *you*.

And you contain multitudes as you will see when you sift, winnow and reimagine yourself, and your capacity for intimacy. We wish you an amazing journey as you dive into this particular river of wondering.

We are beyond what words can articulate.

What we've been learning as we meander along creating this particular guidebook is this: relational intimacy is a complex and interwoven way of being/knowing/responding that doesn't fit into the binary boxes so inherent in the English language and dominant culture. We did our best here with our own growing ways of knowing.

For instance even the language "me and/or you" doesn't describe us accurately because we contain every living being that we have touched and has touched us. We are not separate. We are an amalgam.

We want to acknowledge the limitations of our language in articulating a way of knowing that goes so far beyond it. Even the sky is not the limit of where we can take relational intimacy, relational knowing. It's in the air we breathe. The Mother we walk on.

This guidebook is a beginning place, a jumping off, not a complete anything. Not a finish line. Take what you learn forward, use this as a space to create something new. We send these questions, prompts and images off to you with our deepest blessing.

We are with you on this journey. Side by side. Together, even when apart.

Find your Own Way

Here's our suggestion on how to wind your way through this exploration.

Ultimately, please feel free to meander through any way you like. It is yours to explore. Perhaps think of these ideas as a starting place and then *find your own way!*

(If you are using this workbook in tandem with the Shared Guidebook, set this book down and amble through the "How to" section there as your next step!)

1 TAKE YOUR TIME.
Give each question at least a week.

Sit down with a cup of tea or a cool glass of water and some carved out time to explore the pages. We recommend starting out with a minimum of 15 minutes of writing.

Let the pen move across the page without thinking too much. Keep the ink flowing and find a rhythm that taps a well deeper than the conscious mind. Let the prompts guide you, but not stifle you. You can start with the first prompt or allow yourself to be drawn across the page in any way that suits you.

2 LET THINGS SIMMER AND STIR.
Leave "What's Rising Up?" for the week's end.

After doing the writing session, give yourself some space. Let things simmer and stir during the week following your initial writing. Allow the prompts and topic to live in the background of your days.

Perhaps review and reread the pages a few morning that week, maybe even read your answers out loud so you can hear them as your voice recites them.

Be open to allowing the topic and prompts to pop up unexpectedly and take a few minutes to jot down any insights.

3 WHAT'S RISING UP?
Carve out writing time to record your reflections.

At the end of the week, sit down again. Sift through your writing. Take some breaths. Notice how you feel in your body. Then answer the *"What's Rising Up"* questions.

We recommend a page (spread) a week or bimonthly and we trust you'll find your rhythm. Some folks like to really allow each topic to stew and be stirred for awhile.

Something to consider. Gather a group of friends who like to write and reflect and do a page together once a month. If they say yes, we suggest using our circle process which you can download free from our website. *(https://wonderuprising.com/group-facilitation-guide)*

The ESSENTIALS

Beginnings.

From inception, dark, moist sacred womb
...tending to the fiery needs of the animal of our bodies.
The ever so simple caress of your fingers entwining mine.
"I see you."
Say the soft green brown eyes gazing here.
Our invisible sores are often sharp and sticky if not named and held.

Together.

Can I hold myself?
And can you hold me?
And the world...

It's fitting that all these pages focus on an "A" word.

WHAT IS YOUR
EXPERIENCE WITH BEING

*SEEN, HEARD and
ACKNOWLEDGED*

IN YOUR LIFE?

I wonder and question...

Initial **feelings** that rise up?

What are the **dominant messages**
I've received about this?

What was my **childhood experience**
around this?

How has my **childhood experience**
played out in adulthood?

10

How do I **receive this** from others?

How do I **give or offer** this to others?

How do I **offer this quality** to myself (my inner life)?

What is the part of this **I don't want to talk about?**
What are the stories I am telling myself?

What does your **heart** want?

WHAT AM I SEEING
FRESHLY?

WHAT WAY OF BEING
DO I WANT TO ENHANCE?

WHAT'S
RISING
UP?

WHAT IS HELPFUL
TO IMAGINE?

WHAT AM I
CURIOUS ABOUT?

What practices/actions do I want to consider?

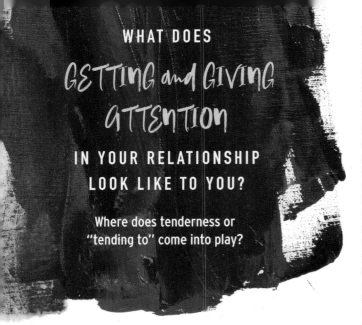

WHAT DOES

GETTING and GIVING ATTENTION

IN YOUR RELATIONSHIP LOOK LIKE TO YOU?

Where does tenderness or "tending to" come into play?

I wonder and question...

Initial feelings that rise up?

What are the dominant messages I've received about this?

What was my childhood experience around this?

How has my childhood experience played out in adulthood?

How do I **receive this** from others?

How do I **give or offer** this to others?

How do I **offer this quality** to myself (my inner life)?

What is the part of this I **don't want to talk about**?
What are the stories I am telling myself?

What does your heart want?

WHAT'S **RISING UP?**

WHAT AM I SEEING
FRESHLY?

WHAT WAY OF BEING
DO I WANT TO ENHANCE?

WHAT IS HELPFUL
TO IMAGINE?

WHAT AM I
CURIOUS ABOUT?

What practices/actions do I want to consider?

WHAT DOES IT MEAN TO TRULY ACCEPT YOURSELF?

I wonder and question...

Initial **feelings** that rise up?

What are the **dominant messages** I've received about this?

What was my childhood experience around this?

How has my childhood experience played out in adulthood?

How do I **receive this** from others?

How do I **give or offer** this to others?

How do I **offer this quality** to myself (my inner life)?

What is the part of this I **don't want to talk about?**
What are the stories I am telling myself?

What does your **heart** want?

WHAT'S
RISING
UP?

WHAT AM I SEEING
FRESHLY?

WHAT WAY OF BEING
DO I WANT TO ENHANCE?

WHAT IS HELPFUL
TO IMAGINE?

WHAT AM I
CURIOUS ABOUT?

What practices/actions do I want to consider?

WHAT PART OF YOURSELF DO YOU ALLOW *OTHERS TO SEE?*

I wonder and question...

Initial feelings that rise up?

What are the **dominant messages** I've received about this?

What was my **childhood experience** around this?

How has my childhood experience played out in adulthood?

How do I **receive this** from others?

How do I **give or offer** this to others?

How do I **offer this quality** to myself (my inner life)?

What is the part of this I don't want to talk about?
What are the stories I am telling myself?

What does your heart want?

WHAT AM I SEEING
FRESHLY?

WHAT WAY OF BEING
DO I WANT TO ENHANCE?

WHAT'S
RISING
UP?

WHAT IS HELPFUL
TO IMAGINE?

WHAT AM I
CURIOUS ABOUT?

What practices/actions do I want to consider?

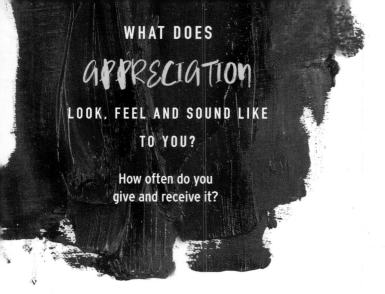

WHAT DOES

appreciation

LOOK, FEEL AND SOUND LIKE

TO YOU?

How often do you give and receive it?

I wonder and question...

Initial feelings that rise up?

What are the dominant messages
I've received about this?

What was my childhood experience
around this?

How has my childhood experience
played out in adulthood?

How do I **receive this** from others?

How do I **give or offer** this to others?

How do I **offer this quality** to myself (my inner life)?

What is the part of this **I don't want to talk about?**
What are the stories I am telling myself?

What does your **heart** want?

WHAT'S **RISING UP?**

WHAT AM I SEEING
FRESHLY?

WHAT WAY OF BEING
DO I WANT TO ENHANCE?

WHAT IS HELPFUL
TO IMAGINE?

WHAT AM I
CURIOUS ABOUT?

What practices/actions do I want to consider?

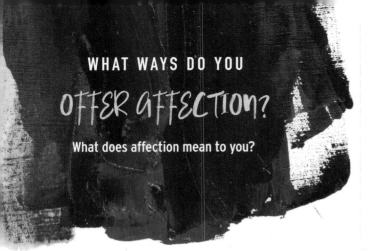

WHAT WAYS DO YOU OFFER AFFECTION?

What does affection mean to you?

I wonder and question...

Initial feelings that rise up?

What are the **dominant messages** I've received about this?

What was my **childhood experience** around this?

How has my **childhood experience** played out in adulthood?

How do I **receive this** from others?

How do I **give or offer** this to others?

How do I **offer this quality** to myself (my inner life)?

What is the part of this I **don't want to talk about?**
What are the stories I am telling myself?

What does your heart want?

WHAT'S
RISING
UP?

WHAT AM I SEEING
FRESHLY?

WHAT WAY OF BEING
DO I WANT TO ENHANCE?

WHAT IS HELPFUL
TO IMAGINE?

WHAT AM I
CURIOUS ABOUT?

What practices/actions do I want to consider?

SHARING the CARE

The delighted fountain that wells up,
spills over, as trust grows.

The deep crevasses and tippy tall mountain peaks of reverence.
The wonderment of being quietly together or apart...
of contemplation and reflection.

Silence, as golden, for good reason.
The floodgates, or the trickling releasing of grief.
The shimmery, star filled, midnight blue of spaciousness.

Me. You. We. Makes three.

HOW DO YOU
GIVE AND TAKE SPACE
IN YOUR RELATIONSHIP?

Initial **feelings** that rise up?

What are the **dominant messages**
I've received about this?

I wonder and question...

What was my **childhood experience**
around this?

How has my **childhood experience**
played out in adulthood?

How do I **receive this** from others?

How do I **give or offer** this to others?

How do I **offer this quality** to myself (my inner life)?

What is the part of this **I don't want to talk about?**
What are the stories I am telling myself?

What does your **heart** want?

WHAT AM I SEEING FRESHLY?

WHAT WAY OF BEING DO I WANT TO ENHANCE?

WHAT'S *RISING UP?*

WHAT IS HELPFUL TO IMAGINE?

WHAT AM I CURIOUS ABOUT?

What practices/actions do I want to consider?

WHAT HELPS YOU
KNOW YOU ARE

CARED FOR
& TRUSTED

BY YOUR PARTNER?

What builds trust?
What has eroded it?

I wonder and question...

Initial feelings that rise up?

What are the dominant messages
I've received about this?

What was my childhood experience
around this?

How has my childhood experience
played out in adulthood?

How do I **receive this** from others?

How do I **give or offer** this to others?

How do I **offer this quality** to myself (my inner life)?

What is the part of this I **don't want to talk about?**
What are the stories I am telling myself?

What does your **heart want?**

WHAT'S
RISING
UP?

WHAT AM I SEEING
FRESHLY?

WHAT WAY OF BEING
DO I WANT TO ENHANCE?

WHAT IS HELPFUL
TO IMAGINE?

WHAT AM I
CURIOUS ABOUT?

What practices/actions do I want to consider?

REVERENCE

(DEEP RESPECT FOR
SOMEONE OR SOMETHING)

HOW DOES REVERENCE
ENTER YOUR RELATIONSHIP?

How do you or could you cultivate this quality
to be in service to your relationships?

I wonder and question...

Initial feelings that rise up?

What are the dominant messages
I've received about this?

What was my childhood experience
around this?

How has my childhood experience
played out in adulthood?

How do I **receive this** from others?

How do I **give or offer** this to others?

How do I **offer this quality** to myself (my inner life)?

What is the part of this I **don't want to talk about?**
What are the stories I am telling myself?

What does your **heart want?**

WHAT AM I SEEING
FRESHLY?

WHAT WAY OF BEING
DO I WANT TO ENHANCE?

WHAT'S *RISING UP?*

WHAT IS HELPFUL
TO IMAGINE?

WHAT AM I
CURIOUS ABOUT?

What practices/actions do I want to consider?

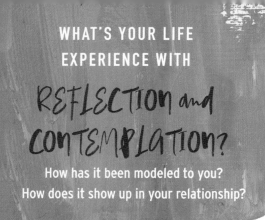

WHAT'S YOUR LIFE
EXPERIENCE WITH

REFLECTION and CONTEMPLATION?

How has it been modeled to you?
How does it show up in your relationship?

I wonder and question...

Initial feelings that rise up?

What are the dominant messages
I've received about this?

What was my childhood experience
around this?

How has my childhood experience
played out in adulthood?

How do I **receive this** from others?

How do I **give or offer** this to others?

How do I **offer this quality** to myself (my inner life)?

What is the part of this I **don't want** to talk about?
What are the stories I am telling myself?

What does your heart want?

WHAT AM I SEEING
FRESHLY?

WHAT WAY OF BEING
DO I WANT TO ENHANCE?

WHAT'S
*RISING
UP?*

WHAT IS HELPFUL
TO IMAGINE?

WHAT AM I
CURIOUS ABOUT?

What practices/actions do I want to consider?

WHAT IS YOUR RELATIONSHIP WITH

GRIEF and GRIEVING?

How has your ability (or not) to grieve
affected your primary relationship?

I wonder and question...

Initial feelings that rise up?

What are the dominant messages
I've received about this?

What was my childhood experience
around this?

How has my childhood experience
played out in adulthood?

How do I **receive this** from others?

How do I **give or offer** this to others?

How do I **offer this quality** to myself (my inner life)?

What is the part of this I **don't want to talk about?**
What are the stories I am telling myself?

What does your **heart want?**

WHAT AM I SEEING
FRESHLY?

WHAT WAY OF BEING
DO I WANT TO ENHANCE?

WHAT'S
RISING
UP?

WHAT IS HELPFUL
TO IMAGINE?

WHAT AM I
CURIOUS ABOUT?

What practices/actions do I want to consider?

INTIMACY is a LANDSCAPE

Flowing expanse

of silvery aqua wetness
Quiet moments of drifting

Cascading, furious waterfalls

Splashing down on rocky outcroppings
Spiral into deep clear pools
Meandering curves

Granite walls that force togetherness

And broad open flat water
Brimming with stillness.
As close as your breath.
What the river knows.

To sit quietly in it and listen to its whisper
Or its howl.

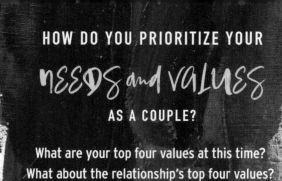

HOW DO YOU PRIORITIZE YOUR
NEEDS and VALUES
AS A COUPLE?

What are your top four values at this time?
What about the relationship's top four values?

I wonder and question...

Initial feelings that rise up?

What are the **dominant messages**
I've received about this?

What was my **childhood experience**
around this?

How has my childhood experience
played out in adulthood?

How do I **receive this** from others?

How do I **give or offer** this to others?

How do I **offer this quality** to myself (my inner life)?

What is the part of this I **don't want to talk about**?
What are the **stories** I am telling myself?

What does your heart want?

WHAT'S
RISING
UP?

WHAT AM I SEEING
FRESHLY?

WHAT WAY OF BEING
DO I WANT TO ENHANCE?

WHAT IS HELPFUL
TO IMAGINE?

WHAT AM I
CURIOUS ABOUT?

What practices/actions do I want to consider?

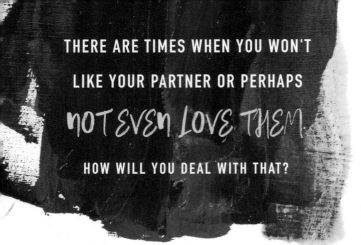

THERE ARE TIMES WHEN YOU WON'T
LIKE YOUR PARTNER OR PERHAPS
NOT EVEN LOVE THEM
HOW WILL YOU DEAL WITH THAT?

I wonder and question...

Initial **feelings** that rise up?

What are the **dominant messages** I've received about this?

What was my **childhood experience** around this?

How has my **childhood experience** played out in adulthood?

How do I **receive this** from others?

How do I **give or offer** this to others?

How do I **offer this quality** to myself (my inner life)?

What is the part of this I **don't want to talk about?**
What are the stories I am telling myself?

What does your **heart want?**

WHAT'S
RISING
UP?

WHAT AM I SEEING
FRESHLY?

WHAT WAY OF BEING
DO I WANT TO ENHANCE?

WHAT IS HELPFUL
TO IMAGINE?

WHAT AM I
CURIOUS ABOUT?

What practices/actions do I want to consider?

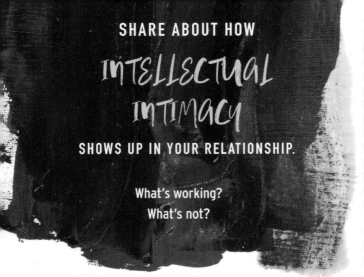

SHARE ABOUT HOW

INTELLECTUAL INTIMACY

SHOWS UP IN YOUR RELATIONSHIP.

What's working?
What's not?

I wonder and question...

Initial feelings that rise up?

What are the **dominant messages** I've received about this?

What was my **childhood experience** around this?

How has my **childhood experience** played out in adulthood?

How do I **receive this** from others?

How do I **give or offer** this to others?

How do I **offer this quality** to myself (my inner life)?

What is the part of this I **don't want** to talk about?
What are the **stories** I am telling myself?

What does your **heart** want?

WHAT'S
RISING
UP?

WHAT AM I SEEING
FRESHLY?

WHAT WAY OF BEING
DO I WANT TO ENHANCE?

WHAT IS HELPFUL
TO IMAGINE?

WHAT AM I
CURIOUS ABOUT?

What practices/actions do I want to consider?

HOW DO YOU EXPRESS

EMOTIONS ?

Share your thoughts and feelings about expressing your emotions authentically.

I wonder and question...

Initial feelings that rise up?

What are the **dominant messages** I've received about this?

What was my childhood experience around this?

How has my **childhood experience** played out in adulthood?

How do I **receive this** from others?

How do I **give or offer** this to others?

How do I **offer this quality** to myself (my inner life)?

What is the part of this **I don't want to talk about?**
What are the stories I am telling myself?

What does your **heart** want?

WHAT'S
RISING
UP?

WHAT WAY OF BEING
DO I WANT TO ENHANCE?

WHAT AM I SEEING
FRESHLY?

WHAT IS HELPFUL
TO IMAGINE?

WHAT AM I
CURIOUS ABOUT?

What practices/actions do I want to consider?

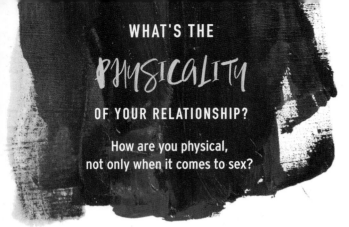

WHAT'S THE
PHYSICALITY
OF YOUR RELATIONSHIP?

How are you physical,
not only when it comes to sex?

I wonder and question...

Initial **feelings** that rise up?

What are the **dominant messages**
I've received about this?

What was my **childhood experience**
around this?

How has my **childhood experience**
played out in adulthood?

How do I **receive this** from others?

How do I **give or offer** this to others?

How do I **offer this quality** to myself (my inner life)?

What is the part of this I **don't want to talk about?**
What are the stories I am telling myself?

What does your **heart want?**

WHAT'S

RISING

UP?

WHAT AM I SEEING
FRESHLY?

WHAT WAY OF BEING
DO I WANT TO ENHANCE?

WHAT IS HELPFUL
TO IMAGINE?

WHAT AM I
CURIOUS ABOUT?

What practices/actions do I want to consider?

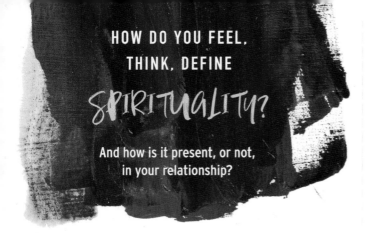

HOW DO YOU FEEL, THINK, DEFINE

SPIRITUALITY?

And how is it present, or not, in your relationship?

I wonder and question...

Initial feelings that rise up?

What are the **dominant messages** I've received about this?

What was my childhood experience around this?

How has my childhood experience played out in adulthood?

How do I **receive this** from others?

How do I **give or offer** this to others?

How do I **offer this quality** to myself (my inner life)?

What is the part of this **I don't want to talk about?**
What are the stories I am telling myself?

What does your **heart want?**

WHAT'S
RISING
UP?

WHAT AM I SEEING
FRESHLY?

WHAT WAY OF BEING
DO I WANT TO ENHANCE?

WHAT IS HELPFUL
TO IMAGINE?

WHAT AM I
CURIOUS ABOUT?

What practices/actions do I want to consider?

RIDING the WAVES

Conflict averse or conflict ready.

Sometimes a mess and sometimes I'm steady
Fight. No flight. Oh nope, it's a freeze.
Is this some kind of undiagnosed dis-ease?
A maelstrom of unskilled language abounds.
So little imagination or creativity to ground.

Are our cultural constructs
of conflict sound?

49

HOW DO YOU FIGHT OR DEAL with CONFLICT?

How is this working for your relationship?
In your life in general?

I wonder and question...

Initial **feelings** that rise up?

What are the **dominant messages**
I've received about this?

What was my **childhood experience**
around this?

How has my **childhood experience**
played out in adulthood?

How do I **receive this** from others?

How do I **give or offer** this to others?

How do I **offer this quality** to myself (my inner life)?

What is the part of this **I don't want to talk about?**
What are the stories I am telling myself?

What does your **heart** want?

WHAT AM I SEEING
FRESHLY?

WHAT WAY OF BEING
DO I WANT TO ENHANCE?

WHAT IS HELPFUL
TO IMAGINE?

WHAT AM I
CURIOUS ABOUT?

What practices/actions do I want to consider?

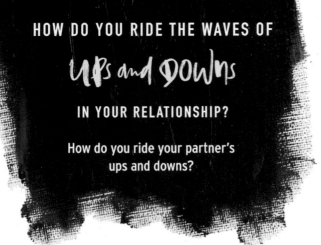

HOW DO YOU RIDE THE WAVES OF

Ups and Downs

IN YOUR RELATIONSHIP?

How do you ride your partner's
ups and downs?

I wonder and question...

Initial **feelings** that rise up?

What are the **dominant messages**
I've received about this?

What was my **childhood experience**
around this?

How has my **childhood experience**
played out in adulthood?

How do I **receive this** from others?

How do I **give or offer** this to others?

How do I **offer this quality** to myself (my inner life)?

What is the part of this **I don't want to talk about?**
What are the stories I am telling myself?

What does your **heart** want?

WHAT'S
**RISING
UP?**

WHAT AM I SEEING
FRESHLY?

WHAT WAY OF BEING
DO I WANT TO ENHANCE?

WHAT IS HELPFUL
TO IMAGINE?

WHAT AM I
CURIOUS ABOUT?

What practices/actions do I want to consider?

HOW DO YOU

FORGIVE?

When? What are you willing to forgive?
What are your strategies for repairing
your relationship?

I wonder and question...

Initial **feelings** that rise up?

What are the **dominant messages**
I've received about this?

What was my **childhood experience**
around this?

How has my **childhood experience**
played out in adulthood?

How do I **receive this** from others?

How do I **give or offer** this to others?

How do I **offer this quality** to myself (my inner life)?

What is the part of this **I don't want to talk about?**
What are the stories I am telling myself?

What does your **heart** want?

WHAT'S
RISING
UP?

WHAT AM I SEEING
FRESHLY?

WHAT WAY OF BEING
DO I WANT TO ENHANCE?

WHAT IS HELPFUL
TO IMAGINE?

WHAT AM I
CURIOUS ABOUT?

What practices/actions do I want to consider?

HOW WILLING ARE YOU TO
BE UNCOMFORTABLE
AND SIT IN THAT DISCOMFORT
FOR A WHILE?

Where do you find the most
comfort in your relationship?
How could you have more of that?

I wonder and question...

Initial **feelings** that rise up?

What are the **dominant messages**
I've received about this?

What was my **childhood experience**
around this?

How has my **childhood experience**
played out in adulthood?

How do I **receive this** from others?

How do I **give or offer** this to others?

How do I **offer this quality** to myself (my inner life)?

What is the part of this **I don't want to talk about?**
What are the stories I am telling myself?

What does your **heart** want?

WHAT'S
RISING
UP?

WHAT AM I SEEING
FRESHLY?

WHAT WAY OF BEING
DO I WANT TO ENHANCE?

WHAT IS HELPFUL
TO IMAGINE?

WHAT AM I
CURIOUS ABOUT?

What practices/actions do I want to consider?

HOW DO YOU

own your own part

OF A CHALLENGING SITUATION?

How do you give and receive feedback?

I wonder and question...

Initial **feelings** that rise up?

What are the **dominant messages** I've received about this?

What was my **childhood experience** around this?

How has my **childhood experience** played out in adulthood?

How do I **receive this** from others?

How do I **give or offer** this to others?

How do I **offer this quality** to myself (my inner life)?

What is the part of this **I don't want to talk about?**
What are the stories I am telling myself?

What does your **heart** want?

WHAT'S
RISING
UP?

WHAT AM I SEEING
FRESHLY?

WHAT WAY OF BEING
DO I WANT TO ENHANCE?

WHAT IS HELPFUL
TO IMAGINE?

WHAT AM I
CURIOUS ABOUT?

What practices/actions do I want to consider?

SEEING
the UNSEEN

So much obscured by our seeing
through eyes that aren't mine.

Or yours.

Systems that have placed us in and under neon lights;
"work" as the master,
money as head of house,
individual success,
nap-taking as laziness.
The list could be pages long. But I won't.

And the irony...
how much nourishment and nurturance the
invisible offers to the soul, the spirit that lies
within and around each of us.

Human Beings that we are.
And without it are we NOT?
The deep inner wellspring runs dry
without the unseen gems sparkling.
To and in each other.

In a culture of masks. To undo.
Remove. Freshly inhabit vision.

EMOTIONAL CARE
(NURTURING AND ENRICHING)

IS UNSEEN AND UNPAID.

How do you place a value on it?

How can it be acknowledged
more often in your relationship?

I wonder and question...

Initial **feelings** that rise up?

What are the **dominant messages**
I've received about this?

What was my **childhood experience**
around this?

How has my **childhood experience**
played out in adulthood?

How do I **receive this** from others?

How do I **give or offer** this to others?

How do I **offer this quality** to myself (my inner life)?

What is the part of this **I don't want to talk about?**
What are the stories I am telling myself?

What does your **heart** want?

WHAT AM I SEEING
FRESHLY?

WHAT WAY OF BEING
DO I WANT TO ENHANCE?

WHAT'S
*RISING
UP?*

WHAT IS HELPFUL
TO IMAGINE?

WHAT AM I
CURIOUS ABOUT?

What practices/actions do I want to consider?

HOW ARE CHORES NAMED AND DIVIDED?

ALL CHORES:

PHYSICAL, EMOTIONAL, SPIRITUAL, AND INTELLECTUAL.

What parts do you play in nurturing the spirit and soul of the relationship?

(Anything that takes time or mental or emotional energy is up for grabs here.)

I wonder and question...

Initial feelings that rise up?

What are the dominant messages I've received about this?

What was my childhood experience around this?

How has my childhood experience played out in adulthood?

How do I **receive this** from others?

How do I **give or offer** this to others?

How do I **offer this quality** to myself (my inner life)?

What is the part of this I **don't want to talk about?**
What are the stories I am telling myself?

What does your heart want?

WHAT AM I SEEING
FRESHLY?

WHAT WAY OF BEING
DO I WANT TO ENHANCE?

WHAT'S
RISING
UP?

WHAT IS HELPFUL
TO IMAGINE?

WHAT AM I
CURIOUS ABOUT?

What practices/actions do I want to consider?

HOW DO YOU TEND AND

EXTEND CARE

TO YOUR EXTENDED FAMILY, FRIENDS, AND COMMUNITY?

I wonder and question...

Initial feelings that rise up?

What are the dominant messages
I've received about this?

What was my childhood experience
around this?

How has my childhood experience
played out in adulthood?

How do I **receive this** from others?

How do I **give or offer** this to others?

How do I **offer this quality** to myself (my inner life)?

What is the part of this **I don't want to talk about?**
What are the stories I am telling myself?

What does your **heart** want?

WHAT'S

RISING
UP?

WHAT AM I SEEING
FRESHLY?

WHAT WAY OF BEING
DO I WANT TO ENHANCE?

WHAT IS HELPFUL
TO IMAGINE?

WHAT AM I
CURIOUS ABOUT?

What practices/actions do I want to consider?

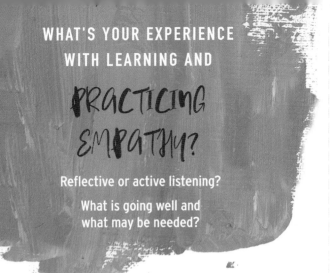

WHAT'S YOUR EXPERIENCE WITH LEARNING AND

PRACTICING EMPATHY?

Reflective or active listening?

What is going well and what may be needed?

I wonder and question...

Initial feelings that rise up?

What are the dominant messages I've received about this?

What was my childhood experience around this?

How has my childhood experience played out in adulthood?

How do I **receive this** from others?

How do I **give or offer** this to others?

How do I **offer this quality** to myself (my inner life)?

What is the part of this I don't want to talk about?
What are the stories I am telling myself?

What does your heart want?

WHAT'S

RISING UP?

WHAT AM I SEEING
FRESHLY?

WHAT WAY OF BEING
DO I WANT TO ENHANCE?

WHAT IS HELPFUL
TO IMAGINE?

WHAT AM I
CURIOUS ABOUT?

What practices/actions do I want to consider?

Sharing of RESOURCES

The *soul* and role of *economics.*

The wee one within that never "is" or "was" enough.

A shadowy darkness that muddies the waters.
And the ancient wisdom of the braided strands
That loosen to liberate
The budding sensuality of *enoughness.*

A tapestry freshly woven with generosity of *sharing and caring*
The pliant weave of offering, gifting and receiving.
The Mobius strip. Flowing, circular.

Taking only what we need.
The abundance of the more than human world
We turn towards
Embracing ritual, reverence, honoring…

Simplicity.

DO YOU HAVE

AGREEMENTS or GUIDELINES

ABOUT HOW YOU SHARE YOUR ECONOMIC RESOURCES?

How equitable is it based on visible and invisible work?

I wonder and question...

Initial **feelings** that rise up?

What are the **dominant messages** I've received about this?

What was my **childhood experience** around this?

How has my **childhood experience** played out in adulthood?

How do I **receive this** from others?

How do I **give or offer** this to others?

How do I **offer this quality** to myself (my inner life)?

What is the part of this **I don't want to talk about?**
What are the stories I am telling myself?

What does your **heart** want?

WHAT AM I SEEING
FRESHLY?

WHAT WAY OF BEING
DO I WANT TO ENHANCE?

WHAT'S
RISING
UP?

WHAT IS HELPFUL
TO IMAGINE?

WHAT AM I
CURIOUS ABOUT?

What practices/actions do I want to consider?

WHAT WAS MODELED TO YOU
as a child
AROUND FINANCES AND ECONOMICS?

What is your "lack" story?

How might greed and hoarding
be a part of lack?

I wonder and question...

Initial **feelings** that rise up?

What are the **dominant messages**
I've received about this?

What was my **childhood experience**
around this?

How has my **childhood experience**
played out in adulthood?

How do I **receive this** from others?

How do I **give or offer** this to others?

How do I **offer this quality** to myself (my inner life)?

What is the part of this **I don't want to talk about?**
What are the stories I am telling myself?

What does your **heart** want?

WHAT AM I SEEING
FRESHLY?

WHAT WAY OF BEING
DO I WANT TO ENHANCE?

WHAT'S
RISING
UP?

WHAT IS HELPFUL
TO IMAGINE?

WHAT AM I
CURIOUS ABOUT?

What practices/actions do I want to consider?

HOW DOES YOUR RELATIONSHIP TO

FINANCES and CONSUMERISM

AFFECT YOUR RELATIONSHIP WITH YOUR PARTNER?

How does it affect all other species on the planet?

I wonder and question...

Initial **feelings** that rise up?

What are the **dominant messages** I've received about this?

What was my **childhood experience** around this?

How has my **childhood experience** played out in adulthood?

How do I **receive this** from others?

How do I **give or offer** this to others?

How do I **offer this quality** to myself (my inner life)?

What is the part of this **I don't want to talk about?**
What are the stories I am telling myself?

What does your **heart** want?

WHAT AM I SEEING
FRESHLY?

WHAT WAY OF BEING
DO I WANT TO ENHANCE?

WHAT IS HELPFUL
TO IMAGINE?

WHAT AM I
CURIOUS ABOUT?

What practices/actions do I want to consider?

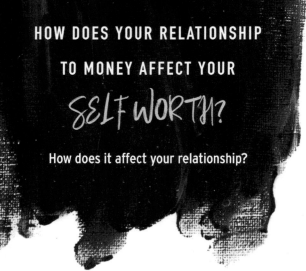

HOW DOES YOUR RELATIONSHIP

TO MONEY AFFECT YOUR

SELF WORTH?

How does it affect your relationship?

I wonder and question...

Initial **feelings** that rise up?

What are the **dominant messages**
I've received about this?

What was my **childhood experience**
around this?

How has my **childhood experience**
played out in adulthood?

How do I **receive this** from others?

How do I **give or offer** this to others?

How do I **offer this quality** to myself (my inner life)?

What is the part of this **I don't want to talk about?**
What are the stories I am telling myself?

What does your **heart** want?

WHAT AM I SEEING
FRESHLY?

WHAT WAY OF BEING
DO I WANT TO ENHANCE?

WHAT'S *RISING UP?*

WHAT IS HELPFUL
TO IMAGINE?

WHAT AM I
CURIOUS ABOUT?

What practices/actions do I want to consider?

a COMMUNITY of BEINGS

Has the nuclear family, or primary partnership,
as #1, served all human beings well?

Or is it time for many to unwind and reweave a more
dynamic, inclusive web.

Collective care, liberation to recreate,
to remake one plus one is two. Into infinity.
Cocooning margins for privacy---not private lives.
A Mobius strip of belonging.
A long house of interconnectivity with spaciousness
for alone time in the simple wilds of the natural world
we inhabit.

Our dancing clay bodies.
The air we breathe together.

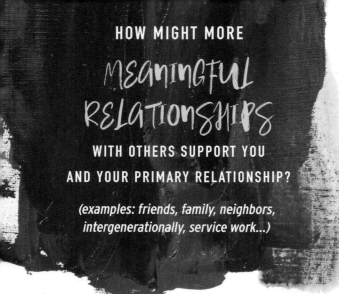

HOW MIGHT MORE

MEANINGFUL RELATIONSHIPS

WITH OTHERS SUPPORT YOU
AND YOUR PRIMARY RELATIONSHIP?

*(examples: friends, family, neighbors,
intergenerationally, service work...)*

I wonder and question...

Initial feelings that rise up?

What are the dominant messages
I've received about this?

What was my childhood experience
around this?

How has my childhood experience
played out in adulthood?

How do I **receive this** from others?

How do I **give or offer** this to others?

How do I **offer this quality** to myself (my inner life)?

What is the part of this **I don't want to talk about?**
What are the stories I am telling myself?

What does your **heart want?**

WHAT'S
RISING
UP?

WHAT AM I SEEING
FRESHLY?

WHAT WAY OF BEING
DO I WANT TO ENHANCE?

WHAT IS HELPFUL
TO IMAGINE?

WHAT AM I
CURIOUS ABOUT?

What practices/actions do I want to consider?

IF WE CAN HOLD THE

naturAL WORLD

IN OUR CONSCIOUSNESS AS A
PART OF OUR RELATIONSHIP,
WHAT MIGHT CHANGE/HAPPEN/GROW?

*(examples: tending a garden together,
watching a sunrise or sunset,
new awareness around the impact
of consumption choices...)*

I wonder and question...

Initial feelings that rise up?

What are the dominant messages
I've received about this?

What was my childhood experience
around this?

How has my childhood experience
played out in adulthood?

How do I **receive this** from others?

How do I **give or offer** this to others?

How do I **offer this quality** to myself (my inner life)?

What is the part of this I **don't want to talk about?**
What are the stories I am telling myself?

What does your **heart want?**

WHAT'S
RISING UP?

WHAT AM I SEEING
FRESHLY?

WHAT WAY OF BEING
DO I WANT TO ENHANCE?

WHAT IS HELPFUL
TO IMAGINE?

WHAT AM I
CURIOUS ABOUT?

What practices/actions do I want to consider?

WHAT MIGHT SHIFT IN YOU,
AND IN YOUR RELATIONSHIP,
IF YOU CONTEMPLATED

IMPERMANENCE + INTERCONNECTIVITY + REVERENCE

FOR ALL LIVING BEINGS
AS DAILY OR WEEKLY PRACTICES?

(example: a blessing on a meal, a thank you
to a friend, a letter to your ancestors past
and future, a ritual space...)

I wonder and question...

Initial feelings that rise up?

What are the dominant messages
I've received about this?

What was my childhood experience
around this?

How has my childhood experience
played out in adulthood?

How do I **receive this** from others?

How do I **give or offer** this to others?

How do I **offer this quality** to myself (my inner life)?

What is the part of this **I don't want** to talk about?
What are the stories I am telling myself?

What does your **heart** want?

WHAT'S

RISING

UP?

WHAT AM I SEEING
FRESHLY?

WHAT WAY OF BEING
DO I WANT TO ENHANCE?

WHAT IS HELPFUL
TO IMAGINE?

WHAT AM I
CURIOUS ABOUT?

What practices/actions do I want to consider?

WHAT MIGHT CHANGE IN YOUR RELATIONSHIP IF YOU CHOSE TO DO SOME KIND OF

SERVICE TOGETHER?

If you already do, share about what happens because of this choice.

I wonder and question...

Initial feelings that rise up?

What are the dominant messages I've received about this?

What was my childhood experience around this?

How has my childhood experience played out in adulthood?

How do I **receive this** from others?

How do I **give or offer** this to others?

How do I **offer this quality** to myself (my inner life)?

What is the part of this **I don't want to talk about?**
What are the stories I am telling myself?

What does your heart want?

WHAT'S
RISING
UP?

WHAT AM I SEEING
FRESHLY?

WHAT WAY OF BEING
DO I WANT TO ENHANCE?

WHAT IS HELPFUL
TO IMAGINE?

WHAT AM I
CURIOUS ABOUT?

What practices/actions do I want to consider?

Four Windows of Wonder

How and what we **know**, and our definition of what it means **to know**, is limited.

When we expand our capacity to see in new ways, we become creative game changers and multi-dimensional problem solvers. We become more inclusive, more effective, and ultimately more capable of *creating a world that works for all.*

In many western cultures, **to know** comes from the thinking mind. From data, facts, calculations, rigorous scientific studies. And yet we have a heart-mind, we have a gut-brain, we have an imagination, and we have a sensing/feeling body. These are all ways of **knowing,** many of which have been diminished and even oppressed.

To limit our way of knowing to only *thinking* **shrinks our capacity to embody our wholeness, to be fully human.**

On the flip side, to embrace these other ways of knowing, to open ourselves up to relearning how to feel, sense and imagine, is to invite our whole selves to the table.

WHAT SENSATIONS DO YOU NOTICE IN YOUR BODY ?

Achy	Sparkly	Suffocated	Hot	Tingling	Smooth
Numb	Breathless	Buzzy	Rigid	Contracted	Warm
Empty	Prickly	Radiating	Throbbing	Shaky	Electric
Full	Stiff	Sweaty	Constricted	Trembly	Soft
Cramped	Bruised	Clammy	Sensitive	Dizzy	Wobbly
Spacey	Pulsing	Relaxed	Ripply	Shivery	Sore
Airy	Flowy	Tender	Tight	Twitchy	Wooden
Pain	Still	Clenched	Contained	Drained	Swirly
Spacious	Burning	Releasing	Open	Slow	
Blocked	Wiggly	Tense	Jumpy	Vibrating	
Pounding	Queasy	Cold	Settled	Dull	

HOW ARE YOU *FEELING?*

STRESSED

Overwhelmed
Tired
Unclear
Foggy
Confused
Exhausted
Numb
Disconnected

Troubled
Fatigued
Burned-out
Embarrassed
Uncomfortable
Uneasy
Discomfort
Discombobulated

FRUSTRATED

Anxious
Disturbed
Dismayed
Disappointed
Disheartened
Restless

GRIEF

Sadness
Depressed
Despair
Downtrodden
Hopeless
Regretful

CONCERNED

Overwhelmed
Confused
Shocked
Stunned
Appalled

PAIN

Agony
Hurt
Lonely
Isolated
Detached
Bored
Unwilling

> *Imagination is more important than knowledge.*
> *Knowledge is limited. Imagination encircles the world.*
> ALBERT EINSTEIN

SCARED

Frightened
Worried
Apprehensive
Panicky
Overwhelmed

ANGRY

Aggravated
Agitated
Annoyed
Impatient

PEACEFUL

Ease
Serene
Tranquil
Calm
Relaxed

GRATEFUL

Thankful
Appreciative
Wowed

TENDER

Affectionate
Touched
Moved
Nurturing
Whimsical

HOPEFUL

Secure
Safe
Reassured

EXCITED

Exuberant
Thrilled
Overjoyed
Amazed
Ecstatic
Enthusiastic
Ebullient
Energetic
Passionate

CURIOUS

Open
Engaged
Present
Resilient

RELAXED

Chill
Rejuvenated
Light
Rested
Renewed
Comfortable

ATTENTIVE

Focused
Present
Engaged
Alert
Clear-headed

PLAYFUL

Joyful
Light
Empowered
Robust
Amused

HEALTHY

Well
Energetic
Fluid
Flowing
Alert
Alive
Lively

In collaboration

CAROL DELMONICO is a passionate questioner, deep listener, and curator of wonder. She aspires to live with reciprocity and reverence for all living beings. On any given day, you may find her dancing, singing, hula-hooping while reading, or meandering the nearby Deschutes River trails, with a wisp of a smile on her face as she breathes in a Ponderosa.

CASEY DAVIS is constantly reimagining the world around her. A cultural questioner, she pours her energy into people and projects that dream up a new story: one that values relationship, with eachother and the land. A mother, a maker, and a mender, Casey finds comfort in strumming her ukulele, sinking her hands into the earth, singing around a fire, moving to the music and time spent in the company of more than human beings.

JESS DEMONTE is a painter and a cook with New York roots. She carries a compassionate curiosity toward all relationships, human and non-human, and envisions stewarding, growing food, and living gently on the land.